ARAB COOKING

EGYPT - MAGHREB - TURKEY
JORDAN - LEBANON

BONECHI

How to read the Flash Cards

DIFFICULTY		FLAVOR		NUTRITIONAL VALUE	
Simple	●	Mild	●	Low	●
Moderate	●●	Moderately spicy	●●	Medium	●●
Difficult	●●●	Spicy	●●●	High	●●●

Cooking times are shown in minutes, e. g. 30' is 30 minutes.

Project and editorial concept: Casa Editrice Bonechi
Series editor: Alberto Andreini
Coordinator: Paolo Piazzesi
Graphics: Andrea Agnorelli
Layout: Alberto Douglas Scotti
Edited by: Costanza Marsili Libelli, Patrizia Chirichigno
English translation by: Julia Weiss

Chef: Lisa Mugnai
Nutritionist: Dr. John Luke Hili

The photographs of the foods, property of the Bonechi Archives were taken by Andrea Fantauzzo.

The landscape photographs are the property of the Casa Editrice Bonechi Archives.

INTRODUCTION

You are about to embark on a fantastic journey of discovery, through the countries of the Southern and Eastern parts of the Mediterranean Basin – from Morocco to Turkey – from an incredible vantage point: their culinary traditions. It is a reconnaissance trip, to learn about the best of this varied, flavorful, colorful, appetizing and above all, healthful cuisine (it uses but few, and mainly vegetables fats).

There is a rich range of recipes including many one-dish meals and some excellent soups, that offer wonderful ideas for making life easier, be it in preparing daily

meals or entertaining guests.

For our tour, we have grouped the dishes by type rather than origin, but further on you will find some hints on how to create complete national menus. Otherwise, let your imagination guide you in choosing the most appropriate combinations for a light lunch, a dinner with friends or a lavish *buffet*. Remember though that, even if eating habits and other customs have been greatly modernized, Islamic tradition as far as serving foods is concerned is quite different from ours. Meals are not served in "courses" as in the west. All the foods, either right after or with the *mezzeh* are brought to the table at once on large,

beautifully garnished trays and platters so that each person serves himself using his fingers. You can easily ignore this custom – hygiene aside – if you feel more comfortable using cutlery. However, if you want to be purists and follow tradition to the letter, prepare finger bowls filled with water and a few drops of lemon juice and aromatized with orange flower oil. And, there is yet another difference: the exquisite, honey-drenched sweets, are not only desserts, they are most often served to visitors and friends at any time, as delightful treats.

For some, Islamic religious laws, make it unthinkable to suggest serving alcoholic beverages with the meals. However, if you do not observe these rules, you will see that our fish and soup recipes are wonderful with dry, flat white or rosé wines, while young reds are excellent with the meats.

If you want to follow custom, we suggest serving water, *carcadé*, or light teas flavored with a touch of mint with the meals.

As to the names of the dishes, we have followed the transliteration systems of the various countries of origin, concerning the vowels (that do not usually appear in Arabic and Middle Eastern writing in general) and consonant groupings.

In many cases, long years of colonial domination have led to an European language being adopted as the unofficial national idiom, not only for phonetic rules, but also sometimes for the names themselves (for example, the Tunisian *Complet* is known by this French name). And finally one suggestion that is never superfluous: read the recipes carefully before you start preparing any of the dishes, check the ingredients, amounts, procedures and any hints. Cooking requires tranquility and confidence. So, *Bismillah!* as they say, which means, *bon appétit*, *buon appetito* and above all, enjoy your meal!

Suggested Menus

Rich and varied, **Moroccan cuisine** offers: *Briouats* and *Zaalouk, Bissara, Couscous Bidaouï, Tadjine bil Hout* and *Tadjine bil'Qoq, Shbouka aux dattes, Barkuk* and for dessert, *Kaab al Ghazal*. From **Tunisia** we suggest: *Marka, Tadjine Malsuka, Odja bil Gombra, Complet, Meshouïya* and *Makroud*. To savor the delights from **Egypt** with *Falafel* and *Ful Mudammas*, try *Malfuf Mahshi, Samak Kebab, Michoteta* and *Balila*. To imagine yourself – and your guests – in a **Bedouin tent**, or on the shores of the **Red Sea**, try: *Kawareh bi Hummus, Kamouneya, Samak bi Tahina, Khabli Palau, Lissan al Assfour*, with *Ghoriba* for dessert. **Turkish cuisine** is sophisticated and the dishes have poetic names: such as *Hunkar Begendi* ("the sultan's delight") or *Imam Bayildi* ("the priest fainted"). And it tempts us with *Hamsi Buglamasi* and *Midye Tavasi Birali, Balik Çorbasi, Cerkes Tavugu, Elmali ve Soganli, Balik, Ilis Domatesli* and *Uskumru Dolmasi*, and it will win us over completely with *Kibrizli*.

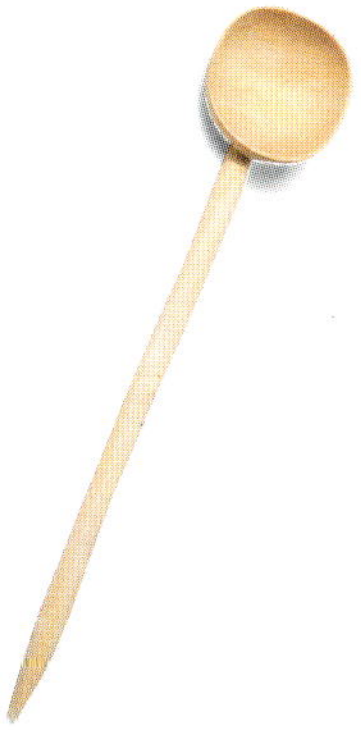

The Utensils

Couscoussière In Arabic the name is *keskès*. This is a double cooker, usually made of metal that consists of a pot (where the meat or vegetables cook in broth) and a covered basket (where the *couscous* is steamed) that fit tightly one on top of the other. You can find them in specialty shops and department stores. As an alternative you can use a saucepan with a fine strainer or colander on top as long as they are both made of metal and can be covered.

Tadjine (or **tajine**) **slaouï** This is the traditional, brightly colored glazed terracotta Maghreb cooker, that bears a close resemblance to a Dutch oven. It consists of a large, low and thick pot for meats and vegetables, and a conical lid. It is traditionally used for slowly cooking foods over charcoal such as stews that get their name from the pot.
In its place you can use a Dutch oven or a pressure-cooker (obviously for stove-top cooking).

The Nutritionist's Advice

The nutritional features of these foods are identical to what is traditionally known as "Mediterranean cuisine." 1) They contain significant amounts of carbohydrates (at least 50%-60% of the daily calorie intake); they are mainly of the complex type, from durum wheat, rice or other grains such as millet or barley, while the simple sugars come from fruit, honey or sugar. 2) Just about the only seasoning oil is extra virgin olive oil, that is rich in monoleic acid. 3) Proteins are obtained from fish or the so-called "white" meats that are rich in polyunsaturated fats, such as lamb, mutton, and chicken. 4) It has a high fiber content from all the vegetables and legumes that are part of every dish except for the sweets.

To complete the overall nutritional picture, we must mention that this gastronomic tradition is rich in one-dish meals (typical of all nomadic peoples), spices (excellent preservatives that are most useful in places where hot climate makes it difficult to store foods for a long time), honey and sugar used in making sweets (and an excellent source of the quick energy that is so necessary in hot summer weather).

Table of Contents

HORS D'ŒUVRES, "MEZZEH", SAUCES AND BREAD

SOUPS AND POTAGES

ONE DISH MEALS AND RICE

FISH

MEAT

SIDE DISHES, SALADS AND EGGS

DESSERTS AND BEVERAGES

Glossary

Orange flower oil Distilled from orange blossoms, is widely used in drops in Arab and Mediterranean pastries (even the famous *Pastiera Napoletana* uses it), because of its delightful, fresh fragrance. You can find it in supermarkets.

Rose water Distilled from rose petals, in addition to being used in many cosmetics, it is often used, diluted to enhance the flavor and aroma of main dishes, desserts and beverages in Chinese, Indian and South-Eastern Mediterranean cuisines. You can find it in gourmet shops and supermarkets.

Brik A very thin bread from Tunisia, usually filled with eggs or various sauces. The dough, known as *malsuka* is used in similar foods such as *b'stila* (or *pastilla*) from Morocco, or the spicy Algerian *dioul*.

Bulgur Kernels of wheat that are steam cooked, dried and ground. You can find it in stores selling dietary products, herbalist shops and more and more frequently, in supermarkets.

Caraway seeds The aromatic seeds of a plant from the parsley family, it is also known as meadow cumin.

Coriander An herbaceous plant that is very similar to parsley, in addition to the seeds (that are actually the dried fruit), the leaves are used in cooking as well.

Couscous In the Maghreb this word is used for both an ingredient and a dish. The ingredient is wheat flour, usually prepared by hand to form tiny, completely separate grains. Today you can find it, ready to use, pre-cooked, in all supermarkets. The dish is usually a strongly flavored meat or fish and vegetable stew, served with the steamed grains (see *couscoussière*).

Cumin The aromatic seeds – whole or ground – of an herbaceous plant from the parsley family (caraway seeds come from meadow cumin). The most common type of cumin is amber colored, but there are also white or black (the strongest) varieties.

Turmeric This impalpable powder is made from the rhizome of a tropical plant that is similar to ginger.
It has a pungent flavor and a bright orange color, and is used in South-Eastern Mediterranean and Indian cuisine to enhance the flavor and color of various foods.

Fenugreek This is an aromatic plant that grows in Asia and the countries bordering on the Mediterranean. The seeds with their pleasant, bitter-sweet taste are used to flavor cooked dishes and salads.

Phyllo This is a very fine dough (of Greek origin) that you can find in the frozen foods section of most supermarkets. It is an excellent alternative to the Tunisian *brik* and similar flake pastries.

Mezzeh (or **mezes**) are spicy tidbits that are served along with or before the meal, and are usually prepared with a great deal of variety and imagination.

Pitta These are round, flat Middle-Eastern loaves made of white or whole wheat flour. When cut horizontally they form a pocket to hold the most varied fillings. Since it has become popular throughout the west, you can find pitta bread in most supermarkets.

Tahin This is a compact sesame seed paste used to flavor South-Eastern Mediterranean dishes, and is available in gourmet shops.

Yenibahar This is Turkish blend of various ground spices and can be found in gourmet shops. In emergencies, you can use curry powder (*garam masala*) instead.

Hors d'œuvres, "mezzeh", sauces and bread

1

BADINGIAN BI RUMAN

Eggplant tidbits

2 Eggplants
1 Onion
2 Cloves garlic
2 Tomatoes
Dried mint leaves
and parsley
Sugar
Vinegar
Dibs ruman
(pomegranate syrup)
Olive oil

Servings: 4
Preparation time: 20'+1h
Cooking time: 25'
Difficulty: ●●
Flavor: ●●
Kcal (per serving): 262
Proteins (per serving): 2
Fats (per serving): 15
Nutritional value: ●●●

Wash the eggplants, slice and sprinkle with coarse salt. Let them sit for one hour then rinse off the bitter liquid they release; pat dry and cut into cubes. Remove the skins from the tomatoes and cut into cubes. Peel and slice the onion and garlic and sauté gently in a skillet with 3-4 tablespoons olive oil. Add the eggplant, the tomatoes, chopped parsley, 1 tablespoon of mint, 3 tablespoons vinegar,1 tablespoon sugar and a dash of pepper. Cook slowly for 20 minutes, then add 2 tablespoons pomegranate syrup. Serve lukewarm with *pitta* or similar bread (see *Khubz* page 21).

200 g/ 8 oz Sesame seeds
100 g/ 4 oz Coriander seeds
50 g/ 2 oz Hazelnuts
50 g/ 2 oz Cumin seeds
Arab bread, for serving
Olive oil

Servings: 4
Preparation time: 25′
Cooking time: 1h
Difficulty: ●
Flavor: ●●
Kcal (per serving): 624
Proteins (per serving): 15
Fats (per serving): 17
Nutritional value: ●●●

Dukkah

Sesame and coriander dip

Toast the seeds along with the hazelnuts in a moderate oven (140 °C/ 280 °F) for about an hour. Chop finely – take care not to pulverize them – in the food processor with a dash of salt and pepper. Put the *dukkah* into a serving bowl. Dip a small of piece of bread (see *Khubz* page 21) into olive oil and then into the *dukkah*.

BRIOUATS

Stuffed sweet and sour pastry fingers

1 Finely chop the onion and sauté it gently in a skillet with 4 tablespoons olive oil; take care that it does not brown. Add the meat and brown it slowly for about 10 minutes.

2 Add the chopped herbs, salt and pepper, half a teaspoon of paprika, a pinch of ginger and a teaspoon of cinnamon. Blend in the eggs, stir quickly and turn off the flame.

3 Roll out the pastry dough quite thinly, cut it into squares measuring 10 cm (4 inches) on a side; brush the edges with melted butter.

4 Place a teaspoon of the meat mixture on each square, roll them up and press down the ends to seal. Fry the *briouats* in hot oil, drain on paper towels; sprinkle with sugar and cinnamon and serve very hot.

250 g/ 8 oz Flake pastry	Ground ginger	Servings: 4	Fats (per serving): 49
350 g/ 13 oz Chopped beef	Parsley, coriander and chervil	Preparation time: 40′	Nutritional value: ●●●
1 Onion	Sugar	Cooking time: 35′	
2 Eggs, slightly beaten	60 g/ 2 oz Butter	Difficulty: ●●	
Ground cinnamon	Olive oil	Flavor: ●●	
Paprika		Kcal (per serving): 696	
		Proteins (per serving): 27	

250 g/ 8 oz Dried fava beans
1 Onion
Flour
Baking powder
1 Clove garlic
Cumin
Parsley
Green salad, for garnish
Tahin
Olive oil

Servings:	4
Prep. time:	20'+20'+5/6h
Cooking time:	20'
Difficulty:	●●
Flavor:	●●
Kcal (per serving):	482
Proteins (per serving):	18
Fats (per serving):	18
Nutritional value:	●●●

Falafel or Ta'amia

Fava bean croquettes

1 Clean the beans by removing the thin skin and soak in water for 5-6 hours. Put them in the blender along with the sliced onion, 1 sprig parsley, the garlic, a teaspoon of cumin and a pinch of baking powder.

1

2 Place the mixture into a bowl and thicken with a couple of tablespoons flour if necessary. Shape into walnut sized balls and set aside for 20 minutes. Coat with flour and fry in hot oil until golden. Drain on paper towels. Place on a tray and serve hot with *tahin* and green salad.

2

250 g/ 8 oz Dried fava beans
2 Cloves garlic
Cumin
Parsley
2 Hard boiled eggs
2 Green onions
1 Lemon
Olive oil

Servings: 4
Preparation time: 30'+5/6h
Cooking time: 2h 40'
Difficulty: ●
Flavor: ●●
Kcal (per serving): 427
Proteins (per serving): 19
Fats (per serving): 22
Nutritional value: ●●●

FUL MUDAMMAS

Fava bean salad

Soak the beans for 5-6 hours; drain and put into a pot filled with cold water. Gradually bring to the boil and then simmer for about 2 and ½ hours. Drain. In a salad bowl combine the beans with the crushed garlic, salt and lemon juice. Set aside for 15 minutes and serve lukewarm with onion rings, chopped parsley, cumin, pepper, olive oil and sliced hardboiled eggs on the side so that each guest can choose his or her condiments.

FATAYER

Miniature spinach rolls

For the dough:
250 g/ 8 oz Flour
50 g/ 2 oz Butter
2 Teaspoons baking powder
Olive oil

For the filling:
1 kg/ 2 lbs. Fresh spinach
1 Onion
Pine nuts
30 g/ 1 oz Butter

Servings: 6
Preparation time: 40'+1h
Cooking time: 25'
Difficulty: ●●
Flavor: ●●
Kcal (per serving): 841
Proteins (per serving): 67
Fats (per serving): 42
Nutritional value: ●●●

1 Combine the flour with 2 tablespoons olive oil, the baking powder, and butter; knead. Add enough water to make an elastic dough. Set aside for 1 hour.

2 Roll out the dough to a thickness of 5 mm (¼ inch); use a glass or cookie cutter to make circles about 4 cm (still about 2 inches) in diameter.

3 Clean the spinach, then chop it. Finely chop the onion, melt the butter in a skillet, add the onion and sauté it gently. Add the spinach, 1 tablespoon pine nuts, salt and pepper, stir and cook for about 3-4 minutes.

4 Place one tablespoon of the spinach on each circle of dough, fold over into a triangle, press down with your fingers to seal the edges. Bake the *fatayer* at 200 °C/ 400 °F for about 20 minutes and serve hot.

HAMSI BUGLAMASI

Anchovies with lemon

Gut, bone and rinse the anchovies. Grease a pan with olive oil. Arrange the anchovies, in rays, sprinkle with salt and pepper, and chopped parsley, continue making layers, and top with lemon juice and with 5-6 tablespoons olive oil. Cook over a medium flame for 8-10 minutes, and let cool. You can also bake them in the oven at 180 °C/ 350 °F for 15 minutes. Make sure to cover the oven dish with aluminum foil.

800 g/ 1 ½ lbs. Fresh anchovies
1 Lemon
Parsley
Olive oil

Servings: 4
Preparation time: 20′
Cooking time: 10′
Difficulty: ●●
Flavor: ●●
Kcal (per serving): 332
Proteins (per serving): 30
Fats (per serving): 21
Nutritional value: ●●●

HULBA

Fenugreek sauce

Soak the fenugreek for 4-5 hours; drain the seeds well and dry them. Clean the peppers, remove the seeds and stems. Place the seeds, peppers, garlic, onions and tomato in the blender along with a pinch of cardamom, and a sprig of fresh coriander leaves. Put the blended mixture into a bowl and add ½ teaspoon black pepper, a pinch of turmeric and enough water to make a smooth spread. Serve with toast.

- 4 Tablespoons fenugreek (seeds)
- 4 Fresh hot red peppers
- 1 Ripe tomato
- 2 Green onions
- 2 Cloves garlic
- Freshly ground black pepper
- Cardamom seeds
- Turmeric
- Fresh coriander leaves
- Toasted bread

Servings: 4
Preparation time: 20'+4/5h
Difficulty: ●
Flavor: ●●●
Kcal (per serving): 210
Proteins (per serving): 6
Fats (per serving): 11
Nutritional value: ●●

Fenugreek *or* **trigonel** *(known as* **hulba** *in Yemenite language) is a typical ingredient in Arab cuisine; it is also used to flavor breads.*

KESRA

Sesame bread

500 g/ 1 lb. Flour
25 g/ 1 oz Brewer's yeast
Sugar
Sesame seeds

Servings: 4	
Preparation time: 30′	
Cooking time: 30′	
Difficulty: ●●	
Flavor: ●●	
Kcal (per serving): 463	
Proteins (per serving): 11	
Fats (per serving): 1	
Nutritional value: ●●	

Dilute the yeast in a cup of lukewarm water with a teaspoon of sugar. Cover the cup and set aside for 20 minutes. Sift the flour together with 1 tablespoon salt; mound the flour on your work table and make a well in the middle. Add the diluted yeast and knead, add enough water to make a homogenous dough. Divide the dough into three equal parts and shape into 3 round, flat loaves; sprinkle with sesame seeds. Place the loaves on a floured oven pan and cover with a cloth. Let rise for 1 hour.

Remove the cloth and bake at 200 °C/ 400 °F for 30 minutes.

KHUBZ RUQAQ

Fenugreek bread

450 g/ 1 lb. Flour
Fenugreek (seeds)

Servings: 4
Preparation time: 40'+1h
Cooking time: 10'
Difficulty: ●●
Flavor: ●
Kcal (per serving): 461
Proteins (per serving): 12
Fats (per serving): 1
Nutritional value: ●●

Sift the flour together with 1 tablespoon salt, and mound it on your work table: add 1 teaspoon of fenugreek seeds and a drop of water. Knead the dough, adding water as you go along, to obtain an elastic dough; this should take about 15 minutes.

Dust the dough with flour, cover with a dry cloth and set aside for about 30 minutes. Divide the dough into 10-12 equal size pieces and shape them into very thin disks.

Dust each disk with flour and fold in half; place them on a dry cloth and cover with another cloth; set aside for 30 minutes. Open the disks and place them on an oven pan; bake at 220 °C/ 425 °F for 8-10 minutes.

KROSS

Date bread

500 g/ 1 lb. Durum wheat flour
150 g/ 6 oz Fresh dates
Olive oil

Servings: 4	
Preparation time: 40′	
Cooking time: 25′	
Difficulty: ●●	
Flavor: ●●	
Kcal (per serving): 410	
Proteins (per serving): 8	
Fats (per serving): 10	
Nutritional value: ●●	

Blend 3 tablespoons olive oil and a pinch of salt into the flour, knead, and gradually add water – about two glasses – to make an homogenous dough. Divide the dough into 4 equal parts and roll out into disks. Pit the dates and put them through the blender. Spread the date paste over each disk. Put one disk on top of the other, so that the coated sides are joined. Set aside for 10 minutes; now separate the disks. Fry 1 disk at a time in a skillet with just a hint of oil. Turn after 3 minutes and cook the other side.

MIDYE TAVASI BIRALI

Batter fried mussels

1

4

1 In a bowl, combine the flour and a pinch of salt, gradually add 1 glass beer; beat the egg whites until they are stiff and then fold into the flour mixture. Set aside for 30 minutes. Prepare the sauce by combining a handful of sesame seeds, the garlic, a teaspoon of sugar and a pinch of salt in the blender; add the lemon juice and stir.

2 Clean the mussels and eliminate the "fuzz". Place them in a pan, cover and heat over a very low flame until they open. Remove the shells, put the flesh into a bowl. Heat the oil in a skillet.

3 Dip the mussels into the batter so they are evenly coated; fry in the hot oil until golden. Drain on paper towels and then place them on a serving patter, in a rounded heap.

4 Serve hot, with the sauce on the side.

600 g/ 1 ½ lbs. Mussels
200 g/ 8 oz Flour
Beer
3 Eggs, separated
Vegetable oil

For the sauce:
Sesame seeds
2 Lemons
3 Cloves garlic
Sugar

Servings: 4
Preparation time: 40'+30'
Cooking time: 25'
Difficulty: ●●
Flavor: ●●
Kcal (per serving): 521
Proteins (per serving): 24
Fats (per serving): 19
Nutritional value: ●●●

2

3

ZAALOUK

Eggplant salad

1 kg/ 2 lbs. Eggplant
250 g/ 8 oz Ripe tomatoes
Paprika
3 Cloves garlic
1 Lemon
1 Fresh hot red pepper (optional)
Black olives, for garnish
Olive oil

Servings: 6	
Preparation time: 15′	
Cooking time: 30′+ 45′	
Difficulty: ●●	
Flavor: ●●	
Kcal (per serving): 225	
Proteins (per serving): 3	
Fats (per serving): 20	
Nutritional value: ●●	

1

2

1 Wash the eggplants, remove the stems and cook them in the oven at 160 °C/ 325 °F for 45 minutes. Remove, let them cool and peel. Cut them into bite-size chunks.

2 Slowly cook the eggplant in a skillet with 4 tablespoons olive oil, the tomatoes cut into chunks, a pinch of salt, 1 teaspoon paprika, the crushed garlic, and if you like, a bit of fresh hot red pepper. Cook for about 30 minutes. Stir, and sprinkle with the juice of half the lemon. Serve the *zaalouk* lukewarm or cold; garnish with black olives and lemon slices.

Soups and potages

2

Ab Ghooshte Fasl

Legume soup

250 g/ 8 oz Mixed dried legumes (fava beans, peas, beans, lentils)
400 g/ 14 oz Lean lamb
1 Bell pepper
1 Onion
1 Eggplant
1 Potato
2 Tomatoes
Ground cinnamon and turmeric

For serving:
1 Bunch of fresh herbs (coriander, watercress, parsley and mint)
4 Green onions
Vegetables pickled in vinegar

Servings: 4
Preparation time: 35'+5/6h
Cooking time: 2h 30'
Difficulty: ●●
Flavor: ●●●
Kcal (per serving): 257
Proteins (per serving): 30
Fats (per serving): 2
Nutritional value: ●●

1

1 Soak the dried legumes as needed (5-6 hours for the beans; 1 hour for the peas and lentils). Drain and place in a pan with the meat cut into chunks and the chopped onion.

2 Cover the legumes and meat with cold water and simmer for 1 hour. Add salt, pepper, and a pinch each of cinnamon and turmeric; cook for another hour.

2

3

3 In the meantime wash the vegetables and cut them into small cubes, add them to the meat along with a little hot water; cook for a half hour. Serve hot, sprinkled with the freshly chopped herbs, the green onions cut into very thin rings and the drained, pickled vegetables.

Balik Çorbasi

Fish soup

200 g/ 8 oz Grouper
200 g/ 8 oz Gurnard
200 g/ 8 oz Scorpion fish or tub-fish
1 Onion
2 Tomatoes
1 Green pepper
1 Egg
1 Hot red pepper, crushed
Olive oil

Servings: 4
Preparation time: 35′
Cooking time: 25′
Difficulty: ●●
Flavor: ●●
Kcal (per serving): 284
Proteins (per serving): 31
Fats (per serving): 14
Nutritional value: ●●

1

1 Clean the fish, remove the scales, rinse under running water, and cut into pieces. Scald in slightly salted boiling water for 15 minutes. Drain. Filter the liquid through a sieve.

2

2 Finely chop the onion and sauté in a skillet with 2 tablespoons olive oil; add the tomatoes cut into pieces, and the chopped green pepper.

3

3 Cook for 7-8 minutes, salt to taste; add the hot red pepper, add the fish and the cooking liquid; stir and cook 5 minutes more.

4

4 Remove the pan from the stove, and beat in the egg, stirring gently. Serve hot, bread croutons are a good optional with this soup.

200 g/ 8 oz Dried broad beans
4 Cloves garlic
2 Lemons
1 Hot red pepper
Cumin
Olive oil

Servings: 4
Preparation time: 20'+6/8h
Cooking time: 1h+10'
Difficulty: ●
Flavor: ●●
Kcal (per serving): 165
Proteins (per serving): 4
Fats (per serving): 15
Nutritional value: ●

Bissara

Pureed broad beans

Soak the broad beans in water for 5-6 hours. Drain and put in a pan filled with 2 liters/ 2 quarts boiling water, 4 tablespoons olive oil and the peeled garlic. Cover and cook over a medium flame for 50 minutes. Drain the beans, and leave the liquid in the pan; put the beans through the blender and pour back into the cooking liquid. Add the juice of 1 lemon and a dash of salt, stir and cook slowly until it acquires the consistency of a velouté or cream soup. Serve the *bissara* sprinkled with cumin and chopped hot red pepper and the other lemon, sliced.

HARIRA

Ramadan soup

1 Soak the lentils for 1 hour, then add the chopped onion and cook: drain. Put back into the pot with the vegetable broth, 1 teaspoon of saffron and a dash of pepper; cook over a low flame for 30 minutes.

2 In the meantime, put a tablespoon of coriander, a sprig of chopped parsley, the tomatoes cut into pieces, the juice of the lemon, the butter a dash of salt and 1 liter/ 1 quart of water into a saucepan.

220 g/ 8 oz Lentils
Vegetable broth (see below)
Ground saffron

For the tedouirà *sauce:*
4 Ripe tomatoes
1 Onion
1 Lemon
Flour
Ground coriander
Parsley
30 g/ 1 oz Butter

Servings:	4
Preparation time:	20'+1h
Cooking time:	1h 30'
Difficulty:	●●
Flavor:	●●
Kcal (per serving):	313
Proteins (per serving):	15
Fats (per serving):	8
Nutritional value:	●●

1

2

3

3 Cook the *tedouirà* over a lively flame for 30 minutes; stir in 2 tablespoons flour and add the drained lentils. Serve hot.

To make vegetable broth, simmer 1 carrot, 1 onion, 1 stalk celery and 1 tomato in slightly salted water for 30 minutes. Or you can use ready-made vegetable broth.

IMJADRA

Lentil soup

150 g/ 6 oz Lentils
150 g/ 6 oz Bulgur
2 Onions
2 Hot red peppers
100 g/ 4 oz Tomato purée
1 Small container of plain yogurt
Olive oil

Servings: 4
Preparation time: 1h+1h
Cooking time: 1h+15′
Difficulty: ●●●
Flavor: ●●
Kcal (per serving): 363
Proteins (per serving): 12
Fats (per serving): 18
Nutritional value: ●●

1

1 Soak the lentils and bulgur for about one hour in separate bowls. Drain. Put the lentils into a pan, cover with salted water and cook for about 30 minutes; add the bulgur and continue cooking for another half hour. Add a little hot water now and then if necessary.

2

2 In the meantime, chop the onion and sauté it in a skillet in 5 tablespoons olive oil; drain and set aside.

3

3 Put the soup into a large tureen and put the onions on top without stirring.

4

4 Pour the tomato purée into the middle of the *imjadra*, and then the yogurt so that you have three, differently colored concentric circles. Let your guests admire it before stirring and serving.

KAWAREH BI HUMMUS

Trotter soup

1 Calf's trotter
200 g/ 8 oz Dried chick peas
Ground turmeric
2 eggs
Olive oil

Servings:	**4**
Preparation time:	**20'+5/6h**
Cooking time:	**3h 30'**
Difficulty:	**●●**
Flavor:	**●●**
Kcal (per serving):	**466**
Proteins (per serving):	**36**
Fats (per serving):	**23**
Nutritional value:	**●●●**

1 Soak the chick peas for five-six hours. Rinse the trotter and scald it in boiling water for 15 minutes; drain and dry.

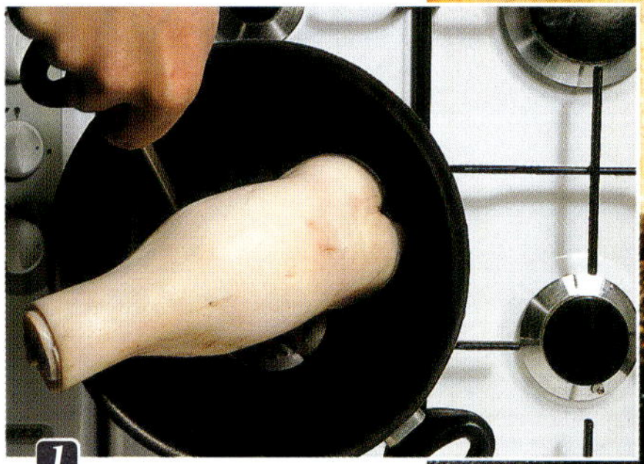

1

2 Brown the trotter in a pan with 4 tablespoons olive oil, a dash of salt and pepper and a teaspoon of turmeric.

2

3

4

3 Add the drained chick peas and cover with water. When it boils lower the flame and simmer slowly for about 3 hours.

4 Remove the trotter from the broth, bone and cut the meat into strips; put the meat back into the pan with the chick peas and reheat. In the meantime, hard boil the eggs (about 7 minutes), shell and chop. Sprinkle the chopped egg over the hot soup and serve.

MARKA

Fish soup

1 Clean the fish, cut into pieces and set aside. Peel and finely chop the onion and garlic; sauté in a sauce pan with 4-5 tablespoons olive oil, 1 teaspoon cumin and the chopped hot red peppers.

2 Add the tomatoes, cut into chunks, salt and pepper; cook slowly for about 15 minutes.

3 Clean the bell pepper, remove the stem and seeds and cut it into strips; add it to the pan, stir and cook 7-8 minutes more.

4 Add 1 liter/ 1 quart water and the fish and a dash of salt. Cover and cook slowly for about 30 minutes. Strain the broth through a sieve, put the fish into it and serve the *marka* piping hot with bread croutons.

1 kg/ 2 lbs. Assorted fish (grouper, weever, mullet, smooth hound, etc.)	2 Cloves garlic	**Servings: 4**	**Fats (per serving): 18**
3-4 Tomatoes	2 Hot red peppers	**Preparation time: 25'**	**Nutritional value: ●●●**
1 Bell pepper	Cumin	**Cooking time: 1h**	
1 Onion	Bread	**Difficulty: ●●**	
	Olive oil	**Flavor: ●●●**	
		Kcal (per serving): 507	
		Proteins (per serving): 39	

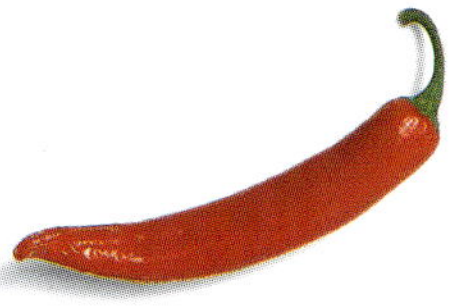

M'DESHESHA

Tomato soup

1 Put the tomato purée into a sauce pan and gradually bring to the boil with 4-5 tablespoons olive oil.

2 In the blender combine the hot red pepper, the peeled garlic, 1 tablespoon caraway seeds, 1 teaspoon paprika and a pinch of salt; then add this mixture to the tomato purée.

3 Add 1 tablespoon coriander and cook over a low flame for about 15 minutes.

4 Add ½ liter (2 cups) water; when it boils add the *couscous*, cook 5 minutes longer. Garnish with chopped coriander and a sprig of chopped parsley and serve immediately.

300 g/ 12 oz Tomato purée
5 Cloves garlic
100 g/ 4 oz *Couscous*
1 Dried hot red pepper
Caraway seeds
Coriander seeds
Paprika
Parsley
Olive oil

Servings: 4
Preparation time: 15'
Cooking time: 30'
Difficulty: ●
Flavor: ●●●
Kcal (per serving): 302
Proteins (per serving): 6
Fats (per serving): 16
Nutritional value: ●●

SHURBA AL-IMMA

Rice soup with meatballs

500 g/ 1 lb. Lean chopped lamb or beef
100 g/ 4 oz Rice
2 Onions
2 Cloves garlic
Cinnamon
Parsley
Flour
Vegetable broth (see page 31)
Olive oil

Servings: 4	
Preparation time: 30'	
Cooking time: 1h 30'	
Difficulty: ●●	
Flavor: ●●	
Kcal (per serving): 393	
Proteins (per serving): 28	
Fats (per serving): 16	
Nutritional value: ●●●	

Prepare 2 liters (2 quarts) vegetable broth flavored with ½ teaspoon of ground cinnamon. In the meantime, chop the onion and garlic and blend it into the chopped meat along with salt and pepper, and a pinch of ground cinnamon. Shape into walnut-sized meatballs; coat with flour and fry in very hot oil for about 5 minutes, drain on paper towels and put the meatballs into the broth. Cook for 15 minutes, then add the rice. When the rice is cooked, garnish with chopped parsley and serve hot.

ONE DISH MEALS AND RICE

3

Couscous Bidaouï

Lamb "couscous"

400 g/ 14 oz Lamb
(or mutton) shoulder,
boned
400 g/ 14 oz *Couscous*
2 Carrots
2 Tomatoes
2 Onions
½ Cabbage
1 Eggplant
200 g/ 8 oz Yellow squash
1 Hot red pepper
Coriander seeds
Ground saffron
(one packet)
100 g/ 4 oz Butter
Olive oil

Servings: 4
Preparation time: 10′+30′
Cooking time: 45′
Difficulty: ●●●
Flavor: ●●
Kcal (per serving): 682
Proteins (per serving): 30
Fats (per serving): 39
Nutritional value: ●●

1

2

1 Cut the meat into stew-size pieces and place in a saucepan with a little less than 1 liter (4 cups) boiling water, a dash of salt and pepper, 1 chopped onion, the cabbage, cut into strips, and 50 g/ 2 oz butter. Clean and peel the vegetables and cut into chunks; slice the other onion, and add them to the meat along with the hot red pepper and a 1 teaspoon coriander. Cover and cook slowly for 45 minutes, then add the saffron.

2 In the meantime rinse and drain the *couscous*. Place it into a bowl, add 1 tablespoon oil and a dash of salt; stir and set aside for 30 minutes.

3 Shape the *couscous* into tiny balls, and put into a strainer to shake off excess grains.

4 Steam the *couscous* in a *couscoussière*, or in a colander with small holes over a pan of boiling water, add a pat of butter now and then and stir. Place the *couscous* on a serving platter, put the meat on top and serve.

To save the time and effort involved in preparing the couscous by hand (steps 2 and 3) you can buy precooked couscous in any supermarket.

İÇLİ TAVA

Rice with anchovies

1

3

2

4

1 Chop the onion finely and sauté it in a skillet with 2 tablespoons olive oil, add a handful of raisins, 1 teaspoon sugar, a tiny pinch of ground cinnamon, salt and pepper.

2 Add the rice and fry it over a lively flame for 1 minute; add a ladle of boiling water; lower the flame and cook the rice for 20 minutes adding boiling water as it tends to absorb. Turn off the flame and blend in a pat of butter.

3 Clean and wash the anchovies, remove the heads and bones; place half the anchovies, arranged in spokes, in a greased baking dish.

4 Put the rice on top of the fish, smooth it down, and make another layer of anchovies, with the tails in the middle. Dot with the rest of the butter and bake at 180 °C/ 350 °F for 15 minutes.

240 g/ 8 oz Rice 1 kg/ 2 lbs. Fresh anchovies 1 Onion Raisins Cinnamon Sugar	70 g / 2 oz Butter Olive oil	**Servings: 4** **Preparation time: 30′** **Cooking time: 1h** **Difficulty: ●●** **Flavor: ●●** **Kcal (per serving): 740** **Proteins (per serving): 38**	**Fats (per serving): 36** **Nutritional value: ●●**

KHABLI PALAU

Lamb with apricots

600 g/ 1½ lbs. Lean lamb
400 g/ 14 oz Long grain rice
150 g/ 6 oz Dried apricots
1 Onion
Raisins
Cinnamon and nutmeg
Saffron (one packet)
100 g/ 4 oz Butter

Servings: 6	
Preparation time: 15′	
Cooking time: 1h 40′	
Difficulty: ●●	
Flavor: ●●	
Kcal (per serving): 611	
Proteins (per serving): 25	
Fats (per serving): 24	
Nutritional value: ●●	

1 Have the butcher cut the meat into bite-size chunks; sprinkle with 1 teaspoon of ground cinnamon, salt and pepper, saffron and nutmeg. Chop the onion and sauté in a pan with 50 g/ 2 oz melted butter; add the meat.

1

2 Add ½ liter (2 cups) boiling, salted water, cover and cook slowly for 30 minutes. Add the apricots, 1 tablespoon raisins, cover and cook for another 30 minutes.

2

3 Cook the rice and drain before it is completely done. Grease an oven dish with butter and put half the rice into it.

3

4 Put the meat and fruits over the rice, cover with another layer of rice. Cover the dish with a sheet of aluminum foil at bake at 160 °C/ 325 °F for 30 minutes.

4

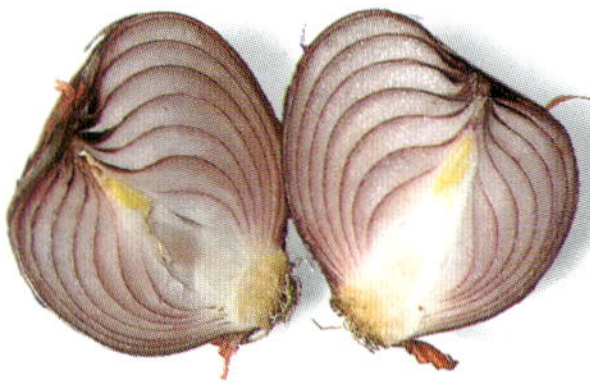

Khoreshfesenjan with Chelou

Duck with walnuts and rice

For the Khoreshfesenjan:
1 Duck,
about 1,3 kg/ 2 1/2 lbs.
1 Onion
200 g/ 8 oz Shelled walnuts
Sugar, Cinnamon
Pomegranate juice
1 Pomegranate,
1 Lemon
100 g/ 4 oz Butter

For the Chelou:
400 g/ 14 oz Rice
4-5 Potatoes
60 g/ 2 oz Butter
Corn oil

Khoreshfesenjan:

Preparation time: 35′
Cooking time: 2h 15′
Difficulty: ●●●
Flavor: ●●

Chelou:

Preparation time: 20′
Cooking time: 20′
Difficulty: ●●
Flavor: ●●

Servings: 4
Kcal (per serving): 932
Proteins (per serving): 45
Fats (per serving): 45
Nutritional value: ●●●

1

1 Clean and dress the duck, remove the head and feet; singe it, then rinse and dry. Rub it inside and out with a mixture of salt and pepper. Brown the duck in a pan with half the butter; remove it and set it aside, keeping it hot.

2

2 Drain the excess fat from the pan, melt the remaining butter and gently sauté the finely chopped onion. Add the chopped walnuts, 1 glass of pomegranate juice, 2 tablespoons sugar and 2 teaspoons ground cinnamon.

3

3 When this mixture reaches the boil, add the duck and cook slowly for 2 hours, basting with lemon juice and its own gravy now and then. Cut the duck into 4 to 6 pieces and place on a serving platter.

4

4 Skim the fat from the drippings and heat, add the pomegranate seeds, pour this over the duck and serve immediately with the *chelou* (see below).

5

5 Peel the potatoes and slice them into circles; place them in a buttered pan with a dash of salt.

6 Put the rice on top of the potatoes with a squiggle of oil and dot with the rest of the butter. Cover with hot water, put the lid on the pan and cook over a very low flame for 20 minutes. Turn onto the serving dish with the *khoreshfesenjan* and serve.

LISSAN AL ASSFOUR

Stewed lamb with egg barley

1 Clean the onions, slice thinly and sauté gently in a skillet with four tablespoons olive oil; cut the meat into bite-size chunks and brown it with the onions.

1

2

2 Add a dash each of salt and pepper, and one teaspoon ground cinnamon, cover and cook slowly for 15 minutes.

3

3 Moisten with 2 glasses of hot broth and continue cooking covered over a moderate flame for 1 hour.

4

4 Add 2 more ladles of broth, when it reaches the boil again, add the egg barley.
As soon as it is cooked (about 7-8 minutes) serve the exquisite *lissan al assfour* with grated *pecorino* cheese.

700 g/ 1 ½ lbs. Lean boned lamb	Servings: 4
250 g/ 8 oz Egg barley	Preparation time: 10′
2 Onions	Cooking time: 1h 40′
Cinnamon	Difficulty: ●●
Aged *pecorino* cheese	Flavor: ●●
Olive oil	Kcal (per serving): 559
Vegetable broth (see page 31)	Proteins (per serving): 45
	Fats (per serving): 23
	Nutritional value: ●●

Matisha Mahsheeya

Tomatoes stuffed with rice

4 Ripe tomatoes
350 g/ 13 oz Long grain rice
1 Onion
1 Carrot
Parsley
4-6 Radishes
Ground hot red pepper
Cayenne pepper
1 Lemon
Vegetable broth (see page 31)
Olive oil

Servings: 4
Preparation time: 40'+2/3h
Cooking time: 40'
Difficulty: ●●
Flavor: ●●
Kcal (per serving): 523
Proteins (per serving): 8
Fats (per serving): 16
Nutritional value: ●

1 Wash the tomatoes, cut off the "lids" and set aside; scoop out the insides, and salt lightly.

2 Gently sauté the sliced onion and the carrot (cut into cubes), in a skillet with 4-5 tablespoons olive oil for about 30 minutes.

3 Boil the rice in the vegetable broth (20 minutes), drain, add a squiggle of olive oil and set aside to cool.

4 Slice the radishes thinly, add them to the rice with the sautéed carrot and onion, a sprig of chopped parsley, grated lemon zest and the lemon juice, a pinch each of salt, Cayenne pepper and ground hot red pepper. Fill the tomatoes with the rice mixture, refrigerate for 2-3 hours, put the "lids" on the tomatoes before serving.

1

2

3

4

MEGADDARA

Rice and lentils

400 g/ 14 oz Rice
250 g/ 8 oz Red lentils
1 Onion
Olive oil

Servings: 4
Preparation time: 10'+1h
Cooking time: 40'+30'
Difficulty: ●●
Flavor: ●●
Kcal (per serving): 752
Proteins (per serving): 23
Fats (per serving): 17
Nutritional value: ●●

Soak for lentils for barely 1 hour, then boil and drain them; set aside the cooking liquid. Clean the onion, slice it thinly and sauté gently in a skillet with 5 tablespoons olive oil; drain and set aside; keep hot. Sauté the rice in the same oil until it is translucent, add the hot water from the lentils, salt and pepper and cook for about 20 minutes. Drain the rice and turn it onto a serving platter, shaping it into a dome, with the lentils and onions in the middle. Serve immediately.

Morg Polo

Chicken with rice

Clean and finely chop the onion; sauté it gently in a skillet with 3 tablespoons olive oil; add the chicken legs and brown them with a pinch of salt and pepper. Add the coarsely chopped apricots, 1 tablespoon raisins and 1 tablespoon ground cinnamon. Cover with hot water, put the lid on the pan and cook slowly for about 30 minutes. Cook the rice until it is *al dente*, drain and place it in a buttered baking dish. Arrange the chicken legs and sauce with the fruits on top. Cover with a sheet of aluminum foil and bake at 150 °C/ 300 °F for 20 minutes.

4 Chicken legs
200 g/ 8 oz Rice
1 Onion
100 g/ 4 oz Dried apricots
Raisins
Cinnamon
30 g/ 1 oz Butter
Olive oil

Servings: 4
Preparation time: 20′
Cooking time: 1h 10′
Difficulty: ●●
Flavor: ●●
Kcal (per serving): 492
Proteins (per serving): 5
Fats (per serving): 19
Nutritional value: ●

PILAF

Rice and lamb

Cut the liver or meat into bite size chunks and brown in a pan with 30 g/ 1 oz melted butter, the chopped green onion and 1 tablespoon each of raisins and pine nuts, a dash of salt and a touch of *yenibahar*. Pour 1 liter/ 1 quart of broth over the meat, cover and cook slowly. In the meantime, sauté the rice over a medium flame in the rest of the butter, for 20 minutes stirring constantly. Add the lamb, cook over a low flame for another 20 minutes. Turn off the flame and put a weight over the lid to keep it tightly closed; wait 20 minutes before serving.

500 g/ 1 lb. Rice
200 g/ 8 oz Lamb liver, or lean meat
1 Green onion
Raisins and pine nuts
Yenibahar
Vegetable broth (see page 31)
80 g/ 3 oz Butter

Servings: 6
Preparation time: 20′+20′
Cooking time: 50′
Difficulty: ●●
Flavor: ●●
Kcal (per serving): 668
Proteins (per serving): 19
Fats (per serving): 25
Nutritional value: ●●

PILAF MAHAMMER

Rice as a side dish

600 g/ 1½ lbs. Patna
or similar rice
150 g/ 6 oz Butter

Servings: 6
Preparation time: 5′
Cooking time: 40′
Difficulty: ●
Flavor: ●
Kcal (per serving): 558
Proteins (per serving): 7
Fats (per serving): 22
Nutritional value: ●●●

1 Slowly melt the butter in a saucepan, do not let it smoke; add half the rice and toast it over a lively flame until it becomes translucent.

2 Add the remaining rice and cover with hot, salted water. Cook slowly for 20 minutes and drain. Half the grains will be white and half brown, creating an attractive effect. Serve the rice with meat or fish, or alone with stewed dried fruits.

Ruzz bi Shairié

Rice and noodles

400 g/ 14 oz Long grain rice
250 g/ 8 oz *Capelli d'angelo* (very fine noodles)
100 g/ 4 oz Butter

Servings: 4
Preparation time: 10'
Cooking time: 30'
Difficulty: ●
Flavor: ●
Kcal (per serving): 784
Proteins (per serving): 14
Fats (per serving): 22
Nutritional value: ●●●

Slowly melt the butter in a saucepan; break up the pasta, and add it to the butter along with the rice, cook for a few minutes, then cover with salted, boiling water. Put the lid on the pan and cook over a lively flame for 5 minutes; lower the flame and continue cooking until the rice is done. Turn off the flame, remove the lid and cover the pan with a clean dishcloth. Wait another 5 minutes before serving. This is an excellent side dish for meats, fish or vegetables.

Fish

4

800g / 1 ¼ lbs. Swordfish, 3-4 slices
Cumin
Ground hot red pepper

For the *testira* (fried vegetables):
1 kg/ 2 lbs. Potatoes
4 Eggs
4 Tomatoes
2 Bell Peppers
4 Fresh hot red peppers
Vegetable oil for frying

Servings: 4
Preparation time: 25′+15′
Cooking time: 40′
Difficulty: ●●
Flavor: ●●
Kcal (per serving): 859
Proteins (per serving): 61
Fats (per serving): 42
Nutritional value: ●●●

COMPLET

Fried swordfish with vegetables

Sprinkle the swordfish slices with salt and pepper, hot red pepper and cumin; set aside for 15 minutes, then cut into evenly sized pieces. In the meantime, peel the potatoes and slice, fry them in hot oil drain, salt lightly andset aside, keeping them warm. Wash, clean and dry the peppers and tomatoes; cut them into chunks and fry with the hot red peppers; set aside and keep warm. Beat the eggs, and in another pan, make miniature omelets, salt lightly and cut them into narrow strips. Quickly sauté the fish in the omelet pan and serve, lightly salted, along with the vegetables and omelets.

ELMALI VE SOGANLI BALIK

Fish with apples

1

2

1 Peel and slice the apples, arrange half in a greased oven dish. Clean the onions, slice and arrange them on top of the apples; put the codfish slices on top with a bay leaf on each slice.

2 Slice the other onion and arrange the slices on top of the fish, and finish with a layer of apple slices. Season with salt, pepper and a squiggle of olive oil. Bake at 160 °C/ 325 °F for 40 minutes.

700 g/ 1 ½ lbs. Codfish, 4 slices
4-5 Granny Smith Apples
2 Onions
2 Potatoes
2 Carrots
Bay leaves
1 Small container of plain yogurt
Olive oil

Servings: 4
Preparation time: 30′
Cooking time: 50′
Difficulty: ●●
Flavor: ●●
Kcal (per serving): 522
Proteins (per serving): 31
Fats (per serving): 17
Nutritional value: ●●

3

3 In the meantime, boil the potatoes and carrots; peel and slice the potatoes; slice them. Arrange them on a serving dish and top with yogurt; put the baked fish with the apple slices alongside of the vegetables and serve.

Ilis Domatesli

Swordfish with tomatoes

800 g/ 1 ½ lbs. Swordfish steak, 4 slices
1 Onion
4-5 Ripe tomatoes
Sugar
Parsley
Olive oil

Servings: 4
Preparation time: 15′
Cooking time: 45′
Difficulty: ●●
Flavor: ●●
Kcal (per serving): 381
Proteins (per serving): 44
Fats (per serving): 16
Nutritional value: ●

Clean and finely chop the onion; sauté it in a skillet with 4 tablespoons olive oil. Clean the tomatoes, cut them into chunks and add them to the onions with a dash of salt and pepper, and 1 teaspoon sugar. Cover and cook slowly for 15 minutes. Add the fish and a glass of water. Replace the lid and cook 25 minutes more. Garnish with sprigs of parsley and serve immediately.

Kefta bil Hout B'Matesha

Sardine patties

1 kg/ 2 lbs. Fresh sardines
60 g/ 2 oz Rice
Paprika
Cumin
3 Cloves garlic
1 Sprig coriandor

For the sauce:
500 g/ 1 lb. Peeled tomatoes
1 Onion
Olive oil

Servings: 4	
Preparation time: 20'	
Cooking time: 50'	
Difficulty: ●●	
Flavor: ●●●	
Kcal (per serving): 456	
Proteins (per serving): 33	
Fats (per serving): 25	
Nutritional value: ●●	

Cook the rice and drain when it is al dente. Gut the sardines, remove the bones, heads and tails.
Put the sardines into the blender with a teaspoon of coriander leaves and the peeled garlic. Put the mixture into a bowl and mix in the rice, 2 teaspoons paprika, ½ teaspoon of cumin and a pinch of salt. Shape into little pattics.
Prepare the tomato sauce: chop the onion and sauté it in a pan with 2 tablespoons olive oil add the tomatoes, cut into chunks, salt to taste and simmer for 20 minutes. Add the sardine patties and cook 20 minutes longer. Serve hot in the sauce.

1,2 kg/ 2 ½ lbs. Sea bream or dentrix (2 wholefish)
2 Onions
2 Cloves garlic
Tahin
1 Lemon
Olive oil

Servings: 4	
Preparation time: 20′	
Cooking time: 45′	
Difficulty: ●	
Flavor: ●●	
Kcal (per serving): 389	
Proteins (per serving): 37	
Fats (per serving): 16	
Nutritional value: ●	

Samak bi Tahina

Fish with sesame paste

Gut, wash, skin and filet the fish. Clean the onions, and chop together finely with the garlic; sauté in a skillet with 3-4 tablespoons olive oil. Remove the skillet from the stove, let cook and blend in 3 tablespoons *tahin*, the lemon juice, a little water and salt and pepper. Spread this mixture over the fish, salt lightly and place them in a greased oven dish. Cover with a sheet of aluminum foil and bake at 180 °C/ 350 °F for 20 minutes. Remove the foil and brown 10 minutes longer.

1,2 kg/ 2 ½ lbs. Bass (or other white Mediterranean fish)
4 Ripe tomatoes
2 Onions
2 Lemons (plus one for garnish)
Cumin
Bay loavos
Parsley
Olive oil

Servings: 4	
Preparation time: 35′+30′	
Cooking time: 20′	
Difficulty: ●●	
Flavor: ●●	
Kcal (per serving): 326	
Proteins (per serving): 37	
Fats (per serving): 13	
Nutritional value: ●	

Samak Kebab

Fish kebabs

Combine 12 tablespoons olive oil and the juice of 1 lemon in a bowl, add a pinch of salt and pepper, and 1 tablespoon cumin. Gut, wash, skin and filet the fish; cut it into bite-size pieces and marinate in the oil and lemon emulsion for 30 minutes.
Prepare the skewers, alternating a piece of fish, tomato slice, bay leaf, lemon slice and onion. Cook over a charcoal grill or under the broiler for about 20 minutes, baste often with the marinade.
Serve hot garnished with parsley, bay leaves and lemon slices.

SAMKEH MECHWIYEH BI TARATOR

Fish in "Tarator" sauce

1

2

3

1 Gut the fish, remove the scales, rinse it. Rub it with half a lemon, inside and out; season with salt and pepper and put 2 or 3 slices of lemon into the cavity. Grease an oven dish and make a layer of lemon slices, put the fish on top.

2 Cover the fish with lemon and tomato slices, season with salt and pepper and a squiggle of olive oil. Bake in a preheated oven at 200 °C/ 400 °F for 30 minute.

3 In the blender combine the sesame seeds, bread, peeled garlic cloves, a pinch of salt and a drop or two of water to make a thick sauce. Blend in the juice of 2 lemons. When the fish is done, remove the skin and bone it; serve with the *Tarator* sauce and fresh tomato slices.

1,2 kg/ 2 ½ lbs. Gilthead (or other white Mediterranean fish)	For the *Tarator* sauce:	Servings: 4	Fats (per serving): 13
2 Ripe tomatoes (plus one for garnish)	4 Cloves garlic	Preparation time: 45′	Nutritional value: ●
4 Lemons	100 g/ 4 oz Sesame seeds	Cooking time: 40′	
	2 Slices white bread	Difficulty: ●●	
	Olive oil	Flavor: ●●	
		Kcal (per serving): 432	
		Proteins (per serving): 41	

Shbouka aux Dattes

Mackerel with dates

1

1 Cook the farina in a little salted water for 20 minutes, stirring constantly. Remove it from the stove and blend in 1 tablespoon each of butter and sugar, salt and pepper and half the grated ginger root. Let the mixture cool to lukewarm and then blend in the egg yolk.

2

2 While the mixture is cooling, put the almonds on a baking sheet and toast them at 160 °C/ 325 °F, remove the skins, chop them and blend them into the farina mixture.

3

3 Pit the dates and fill them with the farina mixture.

4

4 Gut the fish and remove the scales, rinse it. Fill the cavity with the stuffed dates and the rest of the farina mixture. Close with toothpicks and place the mackerel in an oven dish; season with 3 tablespoons olive oil, salt and pepper, and the rest of the grated ginger. Pour 1 glass of water over the mackerel and bake in a preheated oven at 180 °C/ 350 °F for 40 minutes. Serve the fish garnished with the rest of the pitted dates and tomato slices.

1 Mackerel, about 1 kg/2 lbs. 100 g/ 4 oz Farina 150 g/ 6 oz Shelled almonds 2 Dozen dates, put half aside for garnish	1 Egg yolk Sugar 1 Piece of Ginger root 1 Ripe tomato, for garnish 30 g/ 1 oz Butter Olive oil	**Servings: 4** **Preparation time: 40'** **Cooking time: 1h** **Difficulty: ●●●** **Flavor: ●●** **Kcal (per serving): 987** **Proteins (per serving): 49**	**Fats (per serving): 63** **Nutritional value: ●●●**

1 Trout, about 1 kg/ 2 lbs.
2 Onions
6 Ripe tomatoes
Curry powder
Boiled garden-cress, for garnish
Olive oil

Servings: 4
Preparation time: 25′
Cooking time: 1h
Difficulty: ●●
Flavor: ●●
Kcal (per serving): 495
Proteins (per serving): 45
Fats (per serving): 29
Nutritional value: ●●

SAMAK MASGÜF

Oven-baked trout

Gut the fish, remove the scales, rinse it. Season inside and out with salt and pepper and olive oil. Place the trout in a greased oven dish, cover with a sheet of aluminum foil and bake at 180 °C/ 350 °F for 40 minutes. While the fish is cooking, grease a pan with olive oil, add the tomatoes, cut into chunks add the chopped onions, and ½ glass water; cook for 10 minutes, then add 2 tablespoons curry and cook 15 minutes more. Serve the fish hot with the tomato and onion sauce, along with boiled garden-cress seasoned with oil and lemon.

Uskumru Dolmasi

Stuffed mackerel

Mackerel, 1,3 kg/ 2 ½ lbs.
6 Onions
Shelled walnuts, pine nuts and raisins
Cinnamon
2 Eggs
Flour
Bread crumbs
Parsley
1 Onion and 1 carrot, for garnish
Vegetable oil for frying

Servings: 4
Preparation time: 40′
Cooking time: 20′
Difficulty: ●●
Flavor: ●●
Kcal (per serving): 932
Proteins (per serving): 48
Fats (per serving): 63
Nutritional value: ●●●

1 Gut, scale and rinse the fish. Clean the onion and chop it finely, mix in 3 tablespoons raisins, 2 tablespoons pine nuts and 1 tablespoon chopped walnuts, a dash of ground cinnamon, a sprig of chopped parsley and a bit of bread crumbs. Add salt and pepper and a squiggle of olive oil. Stuff the fish with this mixture and close it.

2 Dredge the mackerel in flour, dip into beaten egg and then coat with bread crumbs; press well so that the coating sticks. Fry in hot oil until golden, drain and serve cold with fresh onion rings and sliced carrot.

1

2

TADJINE BIL HOUT

Baked bass

1 To prepare the *chermoula*, combine the chopped coriander with the crushed garlic, 2 tablespoons olive oil, 1 tablespoon cumin, 2 tablespoons paprika, salt, the hot red pepper and ½ glass water. Gut scale, and rinse the fish, and then cut it into pieces.

1

2

2 Take 1 tablespoon *chermoula* and blend in 6 tablespoons olive oil, the saffron and 1 teaspoon ginger. Marinate the fish in the rest of the *chermoula* for 2 hours.

3

3 Roast the pepper in the oven, remove the skin and cut it into narrow strips. Place the strips in a greased oven dish.

4

4 Put the fish on top of the pepper slices, along with the tomatoes, cut into chunks, the *chermoula* you used for the marinade, and the other that you blended with the olive oil. Cover with a sheet of aluminum foil bake at 160 °C/ 325 °F for 45 minutes. Serve with olives and lemon wedges.

1 Bass (or other white Mediterranean fish), 1,2 kg/ 2 ½ lbs. 2 Ripe tomatoes 1 Bell pepper Ground ginger	Saffron (one packet) Olive oil Black olives and 1 lemon, for garnish	For the *chermoula:* 2 Cloves garlic Cumin, Paprika 1 Sprig fresh coriander Olive oil Hot red pepper	**Servings: 4** **Preparation time: 30'+2h** **Cooking time: 30/40'+30' (hot red pepper)** **Difficulty: ●●**	**Flavor: ●●** **Kcal (per serving): 492** **Proteins (per serving): 36** **Fats (per serving): 33** **Nutritional value: ●●**

YAKHNET SAMAK

Golden fried bass

- 1 Bass (or other white Mediterranean fish) 1,2 kg/ 1 ½ lbs.
- 2 Onions
- 3 Cloves garlic
- Saffron, one packet
- Flour
- 2 Lemons
- Parsley
- Vegetable oil for frying
- Olive oil

Servings: 4
Preparation time: 15'
Cooking time: 40'
Difficulty: ●
Flavor: ●●
Kcal (per serving): 555
Proteins (per serving): 36
Fats (per serving): 38
Nutritional value: ●●●

Gut, rinse, skin and filet the fish. Salt the pieces, dredge them in flour and then fry them in hot oil; drain, set aside and keep warm.

Peel the onions and garlic, chop finely and sauté in a pan with 4-5 tablespoons olive oil; add 2 glasses hot water, the lemon juice, salt and pepper and the saffron. Add the fish and cook for 20 minutes. Sprinkle with chopped parsley and serve hot, with the sauce.

Meat

5

Barkuk

Lamb with prunes

1

1 Soak the prunes in water for 30 minutes. Cut the lamb into 5 or 6 pieces. Put the meat in a saucepan with 2-3 sticks of cinnamon, the sliced onion, butter, a pinch of salt and 2 glasses of water. Cook slowly for 1 ½ hours. Remove the lamb, set it aside and keep it warm.

- 1 kg/ 2 lbs. Leg of lamb, or shoulder
- 300 g/ 12 oz Prunes
- 100 g/ 4 oz Shelled almonds
- 1 Onion
- Cinnamon sticks
- Sesame seeds
- Honey
- 80 g/ 3 oz Butter
- Olive oil

Servings: 4
Preparation time: 15′+30′
Cooking time: 2h
Difficulty: ●●
Flavor: ●●
Kcal (per serving): 857
Proteins (per serving): 49
Fats (per serving): 45
Nutritional value: ●●●

2

3

2 Squeeze out the prunes, and put them in the pan along with 5 tablespoons honey and 1 teaspoon ground cinnamon: caramelize over a moderate flame.

3 Toast the almonds in a skillet with 3 tablespoons olive oil, and toast the sesame seeds in the oven. Serve the meat with the prune sauce, garnished with the almonds and sesame seeds.

Cerkes Tavugu

Circassian chicken

1 Chicken, 1,2 kg/ 2 ½ lbs.
1 Onion
4 Cloves
1 Stalk celery
2 Cloves garlic
Tarragon
Paprika
16 Shelled walnuts
2 Slices of bread, with out the crust
Parsley
Vegetable broth (see page 31)
Olive oil

Servings: 4
Preparation time: 35′
Cooking time: 40′
Difficulty: ●●
Flavor: ●●
Kcal (per serving): 814
Proteins (per serving): 42
Fats (per serving): 58
Nutritional value: ●●●

Peel the onion, and spike it with the cloves. Boil the chicken with the onion, the celery cut into chunks, chopped tarragon and salt and pepper. Moisten the bread in a little broth and combine it in the blender with the garlic, walnuts and 2 teaspoons paprika. Put the mixture into a small saucepan, cook slowly until it thickens, stirring frequently.

Skin and bone the chicken and cube the meat. Mix it into the walnut sauce along with 1 tablespoon olive oil. Serve cold garnished with parsley leaves.

KAMOUNEYA

Stew with cumin

600 g/ 1½ lbs. Lean beef
4 Cloves garlic
Vegetable broth (see page 31)
Cumin
Parsley
150 g/ 6 oz Boiled rice
Olive oil
Servings: 4
Preparation time: 20′
Cooking time: 30′+10′
Difficulty: ●●
Flavor: ●●
Kcal (per serving): 410
Proteins (per serving): 32
Fats (per serving): 16
Nutritional value: ●

Cut the meat into stew-sized chunks and brown evenly in a pan with 4 tablespoons olive oil; add the peeled, chopped garlic, a pinch of salt and one tablespoon cumin.
When the meat is golden brown, add two ladles of vegetable broth, cover and cook slowly for 45 minutes, until the meat is tender enough to break with a fork. Serve this wonderful stew piping hot over boiled rice with a bit of chopped parsley.

Hunkar Begendi

"The sultan's delight"

800 g/ 1 3/4 lbs. Boned lamb or mutton
1 Onion
2 Tomatoes
3 Eggplants
2,5 dl/ 1 Cup milk
60 g/ 2 oz Flour
50 g/ 2 oz Grated cheese (Parmesan or similar)
Bay leaves
80 g/ 3 oz Butter

Servings: 4
Preparation time: 20′
Cooking time: 1h 15′
Difficulty: ●●
Flavor: ●●
Kcal (per serving): 576
Proteins (per serving): 52
Fats (per serving): 27
Nutritional value: ●●

1

1 Peel the onion, slice it thinly and sauté it in a sauce pan with 40 g/ 1½ oz butter; add the meat cut into chunks, the tomatoes, cut up as well, salt and pepper, and 1 bay leaf. Cover and cook slowly for 1 hours.

2 Bake the eggplants in the oven at 200 °C/ 400 °F for 20 minutes; cool, peel and mash with a fork.

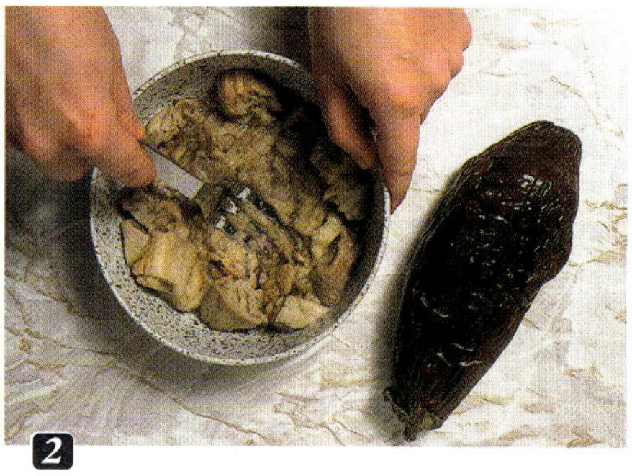

2

3 Melt the rest of the butter in a saucepan over a very low flame gradually blend in the flour and milk, when it boils add the eggplant and cook for ten minutes until it thickens, stirring constantly.

4 Add the grated cheese and stir. When the meat is done, put it on a serving dish and serve hot with the eggplant sauce.

3

4

KIBBEH

Lamb patties

1 In the blender combine the meat, peeled onion and a dash each of salt and freshly ground pepper. Add a couple of tablespoons cold water and blend at low speed.

2 Rinse the bulgur drain and squeeze out excess moisture; put the meat mixture into a bowl and add the bulgur.

1

2

500 g/ 1 lb. Lean boned lam	Servings: 4	Fats (per serving): 39
1 Onion	Preparation time: 50′	Nutritional value: ●●
150 g/ 6 oz Bulgur	Cooking time: 20′	
1 Lemon	Difficulty: ●●	
Lettuce, for garnish	Flavor: ●●	
Vegetable oil for frying	Kcal (per serving): 529	
	Proteins (per serving): 36	

3 Salt to taste, and put through the blender again.

4 Make meatballs and flatten them slightly; fry in hot oil until golden, drain on paper towels and serve crispy hot with lettuce leaves and a sprinkling of lemon juice.

3

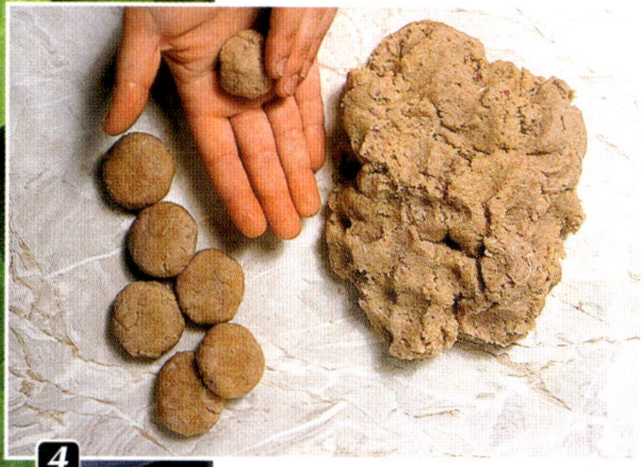
4

Shish Kebab

Kebabs with saffron

700 g/ 1 ½ lbs. Lean beef
Saffron (1 packet)
2 Lemons
2 Onions
100 g/ 4 oz Parsley

Servings: 4
Preparation time: 25′+6h
Cooking time: 12-15′
Difficulty: ●
Flavor: ●●
Kcal (per serving): 183
Proteins (per serving): 37
Fats (per serving): 1
Nutritional value: ●

Prepare the marinade by combining the chopped onion, salt, pepper, the saffron and the juice of 1 lemon. Cut the meat into 5 cm (2 inch) cubes and marinate it for 5-6 hours. Drain and arrange the meat on four skewers, cook on the grill or under the broiler for about 3 minutes on each of the four exposed sides. Finely chop the parsley and distribute it on a serving platter. When the meat is done, place the skewers on a bed of parsley and serve immediately garnished with thin lemon slices.

800 g/ 1 3/4 lbs. Chopped lean beef
8 Eggs
1 Onion
80 g/ 3 oz Cheese (use a semi-soft variety such as *fontina* or *asiago*)
2 Slices of bread without the crust
Vegetable oil for frying

Servings: 6-8
Preparation time: 40′+10′
Cooking time: 30′
Difficulty: ●●
Flavor: ●●
Kcal (per serving): 652
Proteins (per serving): 46
Fats (per serving): 42
Nutritional value: ●

1

KOFTE

Stuffed meatballs

2

3

1 Soak the bread for 10 minutes, squeeze out the water and set aside. Boil the eggs for 7 minutes, shell and put through the egg slicer.

2 Put the onion through the blender, then combine it with the meat, add flaked cheese, salt and pepper and the bread.

3 Take a handful of the mixture – equivalent to the size of an egg – and flatten it; place 1 slice of egg in the middle and close it to make a meatball. Fry the *kofte* in hot oil and serve hot.

300 g/ 12 oz Pizza dough
300 g/ 12 oz Lean chopped beef or lamb
4 Ripe tomatoes
1 Onion
1 Dried hot red pepper
Fresh Tarragon, mint and thyme
1 Lemon
Sugar
Milk
Olive oil

Servings: 4	
Preparation time: 20'+1h	
Cooking time: 45'	
Difficulty: ●●	
Flavor: ●●●	
Kcal (per serving): 437	
Proteins (per serving): 25	
Fats (per serving): 13	
Nutritional value: ●●	

Lahma bi Ajeen

Stuffed rolls

1 Combine the dough with 1 tablespoon olive oil and ½ glass of milk. Shape it into a ball, cover and set aside for 1 hour to rise.

1

2

3

4

2 Chop the onion and sauté it in a skillet with 3 tablespoons olive oil; add the tomatoes cut into pieces, salt and pepper and 1 teaspoon sugar.

3 After 10 minutes, add the meat, stir and pour in 1 glass of water with a little lemon juice.

4 Add the chopped hot red pepper and herbs; cover and cook slowly for 20 minutes. Uncover and cook so that the sauce thickens; turn off the flame and cool to lukewarm. Divide the dough into 4 pieces, shape into disks. Distribute the meat mixture evenly on the disks, roll them up and bake in a preheated oven at 220 °C/ 425 °F for 10 minutes. Serve immediately.

MALFUF MAHSHI

Stuffed cabbage

1 Cabbage
500 g/ 1 lb. Lean chopped beef or lamb
100 g/ 4 oz Rice
1 Onion
2 Lemons
Dried mint
Ground cinnamon
Paprika

Servings:	4
Preparation time:	35′
Cooking time:	50′
Difficulty:	●●
Flavor:	●●
Kcal (per serving):	284
Proteins (per serving):	37
Fats (per serving):	2
Nutritional value:	●

1 Wash the cabbage, separate the leaves and scald them in slightly salted boiling water for 4 minutes. Drain and remove the hard rib.

2 Rinse the rice and combine it in a bowl with the meat, the finely chopped onion, and a dash each of salt, pepper, cinnamon and paprika.

3 Place the meat mixture on the cabbage leaves, roll them into little bundles.

4 Use the remaining leaves to line a pan, arrange the stuffed cabbage rolls on top; cover with water and simmer for 45 minutes; add 1 teaspoon crushed dried mint leaves and the juice of the lemons and cook for another 10 minutes. Serve immediately.

MDERBEL BADINGIAN

Stew with eggplant

- 1 kg/ 2 lbs. Eggplant (about 3-4 eggplants)
- 500 g/ 1 lb. Lean beef
- 100 g/ 4 oz Dried chick peas
- 2 Cloves garlic
- Cinnamon and caraway seeds
- Vinegar
- 1 Ripe tomato, for garnish
- 30 g/ 1 oz Butter
- Olive oil

Servings: 4
Prep. time: 20'+ 5/6h
Cooking time: 1h 15'
Difficulty: ●●
Flavor: ●●
Kcal (per serving): 395
Proteins (per serving): 33
Fats (per serving): 20
Nutritional value: ●●

1 Soak the chick peas for 5-6 hours before you start. Peel the eggplants and cut into thin, round slices. Brown them in a skillet with 2-3 tablespoons olive oil, drain and keep warm.

2 Cut the meat into stew-size pieces, brown in a saucepan with a pat of butter, the chopped garlic, a dash each of ground cinnamon, caraway seeds and salt; after 5 minutes add ½ liter/ two cups hot water.

3 Drain the chick peas, add them to the meat, cover and simmer for 45 minutes; add the eggplant along with 1 tablespoon vinegar and continue cooking for another 15 minutes.
Serve hot, on a bed of sliced raw tomato, drenched with the sauce.

TADJINE BIL'QOQ

Lamb with artichokes

800 g/ 1 3/4 lbs. Lean boned lamb
4 Artichokes
12 Black olives
1 Lemon
Ground ginger
Saffron (one packet)
Olive oil

Servings: 4	
Preparation time: 20′	
Cooking time: 1h 30′	
Difficulty: ●●	
Flavor: ●●	
Kcal (per serving): 391	
Proteins (per serving): 41	
Fats (per serving): 18	
Nutritional value: ●●	

1 Clean the artichokes, eliminate the stems and tough outer leaves. Slice them thinly and soak them in water with lemon juice. Cut the meat into large chunks and put into a pan with a pinch of salt, 1 teaspoon ginger, the saffron and 3 tablespoons olive oil, pour on enough water to cover it all. Put the lid on the pan and cook slowly for about 1 hour. Remove the meat, set it aside and keep it warm.

2 Drain the artichokes and put them into the pan with the meat drippings. Cook over a moderate flame for 20 minutes, adding hot water now and then if they tend to dry.

3 *Julienne* the lemon peel, pit the olives, add to the artichokes and stir; then put the meat back into the pan, reheat and serve.

1

2

3

SIDE DISHES, SALADS AND EGGS

6

Bayd bi Thum

Eggs in garlic

8 Eggs
2 Cloves garlic
Lemon juice
Sumaq (see below)
Dried mint
Boiled baby carrots
Olive oil

Servings: 4
Preparation time: 30′
Cooking time: 30′
Difficulty: ●●
Flavor: ●●
Kcal (per serving): 415
Proteins (per serving): 25
Fats (per serving): 27
Nutritional value: ●●

Heat 4 tablespoons olive oil in a skillet and gently sauté the peeled, crushed garlic along with a pinch of salt and the lemon juice.
When the garlic starts to brown, remove it and cook the eggs, two at a time over a low flame. Sprinkle with a pinch of *sumaq*, and crumbled dried mint; serve with plain, boiled baby carrots on the side.

***Sumaq** are dark red berries, with a slightly tart flavor, they are used dry, whole or ground to flavor meat and fish dishes, or, as in this case, eggs.*

BALADI

Mixed salad

4 Ripe tomatoes
1 Onion
1 Cucumber
1 Green Pepper
Parsley
1 Lemon
White wine vinegar
Olive oil

Servings: 4	
Preparation time: 20′	
Difficulty: ●	
Flavor: ●●	
Kcal (per serving): 136	
Proteins (per serving): 2	
Fats (per serving): 9	
Nutritional value: ●●	

Wash and clean and dry all the vegetables. In a bowl combine the tomatoes, cut into round slices, the peeled cucumber, also cut into round slices, the green pepper cut into narrow strips. Add the onion sliced into rings and a spring of chopped parsley. Prepare the dressing by combining 2 tablespoons olive oil, 2 tablespoons vinegar, 1 tablespoon lemon juice, salt and pepper. Toss the salad, serve with meat dishes such as the *Kofte* on page 85.

4 Eggs
250 g/ 8 oz Anchovies
Flour
Parsley
Tomatoes and lettuce, for garnish
Olive oil

Servings:	**4**
Preparation time:	**30′**
Cooking time:	**30′**
Difficulty:	**●●**
Flavor:	**●●**
Kcal (per serving):	**347**
Proteins (per serving):	**24**
Fats (per serving):	**20**
Nutritional value:	**●●**

Hamsi Kayganasi

Anchovy omelet

Gut the anchovies, remove, the bones, heads and tails. Beat the eggs with 1 tablespoon flour and a pinch of salt. Add the broken up anchovies and a sprig of chopped parsley. Heat 2-3 tablespoons olive oil in a pan, pour in the egg mixture, lower the flame, cover the eggs and cook slowly for about 5 minutes. Use the lid or a plate to help flip the omelet and cook the other side for 5 minutes as well. Put the omelet on a serving dish and trim with lettuce and tomato, or serve with a *Baladi* salad (see page 95).

Imam Bayildi

"The priest fainted"

1 kg/ 2 lbs. Eggplant
4-5 Onions
6 Ripe tomatoes
1 Head garlic
Sugar
Olive oil

Servings: 6	
Preparation time: 30′	
Cooking time: 45′	
Difficulty: ●	
Flavor: ●●	
Kcal (per serving): 194	
Proteins (per serving): 5	
Fats (per serving): 10	
Nutritional value: ●●	

Wash the tomatoes and cut them into chunks; peel the onions and cut them into wedges. Peel the eggplants and cut them into even sticks, peel and crush the garlic. Grease a skillet with a little olive oil and add the onions, tomatoes, eggplant, garlic and 2 teaspoons salt. Put the vegetables into a well-greased stove-to-table pan, add 3 cups water, 1 teaspoon each of sugar and salt. Cook until all the water has evaporated, then lower the flame, cover and cook slowly for 30 minutes. Cool and serve at room temperature. This is an excellent side dish with any of the omelets in this book.

Kukuye Sabsi

Spinach omelet

1 Wash the spinach thoroughly, and chop finely together with a sprig of parsley, and a bunch each of watercress, and mint, 1 tablespoon coriander seeds and the leek.

2 Beat the eggs and blend in the chopped vegetable mixture, chopped walnuts, 1 tablespoon raisins, salt and pepper. Heat 2 tablespoons olive oil in a skillet, pour in the eggs, lower the flame and cook for about 5 minutes until the omelet starts to set; turn it over and cook the other side. Serve immediately, with a lettuce and mint salad dressed with yogurt and a little olive oil.

4 Eggs 1 Bunch fresh spinach 1 Leek 10 Shelled walnuts Raisins Watercress, coriander, mint, parsley	Fresh lettuce and mint, for garnish Plain yogurt Olive oil	**Servings: 4** **Preparation time: 15′** **Cooking time: 10′** **Difficulty: ●** **Flavor: ●●** **Kcal (per serving): 567** **Proteins (per serving): 26**	**Fats (per serving): 44** **Nutritional value: ●●**

MESHOUÏYA O MECHOUÏA

Pepper and tuna salad

200 g/ 8 oz Tuna fish, oil pack
2 Bell peppers
2 Tomatoes
2 Eggs
1 Onion
1 Clove garlic
1 Dozen black olives
1 Lemon
Cumin
Olive oil

Servings: 4
Preparation time: 30'+30'
Difficulty: ●●
Flavor: ●●
Kcal (per serving): 366
Proteins (per serving): 22
Fats (per serving): 28
Nutritional value: ●●●

Boil the eggs for 7 minutes and peel. Wash the peppers and roast them in the oven, remove the skins and seeds and cut them into strips. Combine the chopped onion and garlic in a salad bowl. Crush the cumin in a mortar with a pinch of salt, then transfer it to the salad bowl, and add the peppers, the tomatoes (cut into wedges), the coarsely chopped eggs, the pitted, chopped olives and the crumbled, drained tuna fish. Prepare the dressing by combining the lemon juice and 8 tablespoons olive oil. Pour over the salad and serve with one of the delicious breads (see pages 20-22) to make a full meal.

MATESHA BESSUKKAR

Baked tomatoes

1 Scald the tomatoes briefly in boiling water and remove the skins. Cut them in half and remove the seeds. Season with salt and pepper. Grease a baking dish with olive oil and arrange the tomatoes in it, round side up.

1

2 Sprinkle with 2 tablespoons sugar and a squiggle of olive oil. Bake in a slow oven (120 °C/ 250 °F) for 1 and ½ hours. Serve lukewarm, perhaps as a side dish with *kibbeh* (see page 82).

2

8-10 Ripe tomatoes
Sugar
Olive oil

Servings: 4
Preparation time: 20′
Cooking time: 1h 30′
Difficulty: ●
Flavor: ●●
Kcal (per serving): 186
Proteins (per serving): 3
Fats (per serving): 2
Nutritional value: ●●

ODJA BIL GOMBRA

Scrambled eggs with shrimp

16 Shrimp
4 Eggs
2 Tomatoes
2 Fresh small green peppers
2 Cloves garlic
Parsley
Olive oil

Servings: 4	
Preparation time: 15′	
Cooking time: 30′	
Difficulty: ●	
Flavor: ●●	
Kcal (per serving): 345	
Proteins (per serving): 33	
Fats (per serving): 20	
Nutritional value: ●●	

1 Wash the tomatoes and cut them into chunks; wash the peppers, eliminate the seeds and cut them into chunks too. Gently sauté the vegetables in a skillet with 4 tablespoons olive oil, the finely chopped garlic and salt and pepper.

2 In the meantime, scald the shrimp in lightly salted boiling water, remove the heads, shells and the black vein. Turn them into the skillet and cook over a low flame for 5 minutes. Break the eggs into the skillet, stir quickly, salt to taste and serve immediately with a sprinkling of chopped parsley.

1

2

MICHOTETA

Cheese salad

350 g/ 13 oz Cream cheese (or very thick yogurt)
1 Onion
1 Cucumber
2 Lemons
Olive oil

Servings: 4
Preparation time: 20+30′
Difficulty: ●●
Flavor: ●●
Kcal (per serving): 368
Proteins (per serving): 17
Fats (per serving): 31
Nutritional value: ●●●

In a bowl, soften the cheese with a fork until it is very creamy; dress it with the lemon juice combined with 6-8 tablespoons olive oil, set aside for 30 minute. Clean the onion and chop it finely, cut the cucumber into cubes and mix them into the cheese, season with salt and pepper and stir gently. This salad too, served with one of the breads (see pages 20-22) makes a full meal, or it is a wonderful side dish when served with fish such as *Samak Kebab* (see page 64).

SLADA AL KHIZZOU

Carrot salad

4 Carrots
3 Cloves garlic
1 Shallot
Cumin
Confectioner's sugar
1 Lemon
Orange Flower Oil
1 Orange, for garnish
Olive oil

Servings: 4	
Preparation time: 20'+1h	
Cooking time: 10'	
Difficulty: ●	
Flavor: ●	
Kcal (per serving): 215	
Proteins (per serving): 3	
Fats (per serving): 10	
Nutritional value: ●●	

Scald the carrots for 5 minutes in lightly salted boiling water along with the peeled garlic cloves. Drain, remove the garlic. Cut the carrots into medium-thick circles and place in a salad bowl, with the chopped shallot. Combine 4 tablespoons olive oil with the lemon juice, 1 tablespoon orange flower oil, 1 teaspoon sugar, ½ teaspoon cumin and a dash of pepper. Pour the dressing over the carrots, toss gently and refrigerate for 1 hour. Decorate with either thinly sliced orange peel, or orange slices, and try it with *Kefta bil Hout B'Matesha* (page 63).

PIYAZ

Bean salad

200 g/ 8 oz Dried white beans
1 Lemon
12 Black olives, for garnish
Olive oil

Servings: 4	
Preparation time: 25'+5/6h	
Cooking time: 1h	
Difficulty: ●	
Flavor: ●●	
Kcal (per serving): 306	
Proteins (per serving): 12	
Fats (per serving): 17	
Nutritional value: ●●●	

Soak the beans for 5-6 hours. Then cook them slowly in a covered pot and drain. Take 2-3 tablespoons of the beans and set them aside. Put the rest into the blender. Season with 4 tablespoons olive oil, lemon juice, salt and pepper. Stir gently, then serve at room temperature garnished with the pitted, chopped olives and the whole beans. This is an excellent side dish to serve with *Elmali ve Soganli Balik* (page 61).

Tadjine Malsuka

Lamb omelet

4 Eggs
250 g/ 8 oz Lean boned lamb
8 Sheets of *brik* (see below)
100 g/ 4 oz Dried white beans
½ Onion
Saffron (one packet)
100 g/ 4 oz Butter
Olive oil

Servings: 4	
Preparation time: 15′ + 5/6 h	
Cooking time: 2h 45′	
Difficulty: ●●	
Flavor: ●●	
Kcal (per serving): 811	
Proteins (per serving): 43	
Fats (per serving): 64	
Nutritional value: ●●●	

Soak the beans for 5-6 hours. Clean the onion and chop it finely, then sauté it in a saucepan with 2 tablespoons olive oil, the meat cut into cubes, saffron, drain beans and salt and pepper. Add 2 glasses water, cover and cook over a moderate flame for 2 hours. Remove from the stove, add the beaten eggs and stir gently until it is creamy. Melt 70 g/ 3 oz butter. Grease an oven dish with the remaining butter, line it with 4 sheets of *brik* brushed with melted butter. Put the meat and egg mixture into the dish and cover with the remaining 4 sheets of *brik*, arranged so they overlap, brush them with butter too. Bake at 140 °C/ 280 °F for 25 minutes, then raise the oven temperature to 180° C/ 350 °F and bake 15 minutes longer.

Brik *or* **brek** *are very thin Tunisian crêpes that are usually served filled and rolled; they can be made with eggs or phyllo dough, or plain flake pastry rolled out very thinly.*

DESSERTS AND BEVERAGES

7

160 g/ 8 Sheets of *phyllo* dough (or very fine flake pastry)
350 g/ 13 oz Shelled and chopped pistachio nuts
100 g/ 4 oz Butter

For the syrup:
150 g/ 6 oz Sugar
1 Lemon
Orange flower oil

Servings: 4-6
Preparation time: 35′
Cooking time: 1h+10′
Difficulty: ●●
Flavor: ●●
Kcal (per serving): 818
Proteins (per serving): 24
Fats (per serving): 70
Nutritional value: ●●●

BAKLAWA

Pistachio cake

1

1 Arrange 4 sheets of dough in a buttered baking dish. Melt 70 g/ 3 oz butter and brush it over the dough.

2

2 Cover the dough with the chopped pistachio nuts and then put the other sheets of dough on top, brush with melted butter. Bake at 170 °C/ 340 °F for 35 minutes, then raise the temperature to 210 °C/ 410 °F and continue baking for 10 more minutes.

3

3 Dissolve the sugar in 2 glasses of water add the juice of ½ lemon; simmer until the syrup thickens; add 2 tablespoons orange flower oil, cook 2 minutes longer and remove from the stove. Let cool.

4

4 When the cake is done, pour the syrup over it and cut it into lozenges.

300 g/ 12 oz Pearl barley
Shelled almonds
and pistachio nuts

For the syrup:
150 g/ 6 oz Sugar
1 Lemon
Orange flower oil

Servings: 4	
Preparation time: 15'+3/4h	
Cooking time: 1h+15'	
Difficulty: ●	
Flavor: ●	
Kcal (per serving): 609	
Proteins (per serving): 18	
Fats (per serving): 18	
Nutritional value: ●●●	

Balila

Barley pudding

1 Soak the barley in water for 3-4 hours. Boil it for about 1 hour until tender, then drain and put it into a bowl.

2 Dissolve the sugar in 2 glasses of water and the juice of ½ lemon; simmer until the syrup thickens; add 2 tablespoons orange flower oil.

1

2

3 Pour the syrup over the barley: let cool, the arrange it on a tray and sprinkle chopped almonds and pistachios on top.

3

GHRIBIYET QSENTENA

Sweet turbans

400 g/ 14 oz Flour
150 g/ 6 oz Confectioner's sugar
120 g/ 5 oz Butter
Vegetable oil

Servings: 4-6
Preparation time: 30′
Cooking time: 20′
Difficulty: ●●
Flavor: ●
Kcal (per serving): 868
Proteins (per serving): 11
Fats (per serving): 36
Nutritional value: ●●●

Blend the butter and sugar, gradually add the flour, mixing with your hands, until the dough is firm and homogenous.
Take a handful of dough – about the size of a golf ball – and shape it into a cone – pointed at the top, with a flat base; use up all the dough, and arrange the *ghribiyet* on a greased baking sheet, and bake at 100 °C/ 212 °F for 20 minutes. Remember, they must not brown!

BASBOUSSA

Coconut cake

1 Combine the semolina with the grated coconut, sugar, yogurt and a few tablespoons of cold water.

2 Mix well, and when it is blended, put it into an oven dish, smooth the surface and set aside for 2-3 hours.

3 Dissolve the sugar in 1 glass water and the juice of the lemon; simmer until the syrup thickens. Remove from the stove and let cool to lukewarm.

4 Bake the cake at 170 °C/ 340 °F for 1 hour. Remove it from the oven, cut it into lozenges and pour the cooled syrup over the top. Decorate with slivered almonds or ground pistachio nuts.

400 g/ 14 oz Semolina
200 g/ 8 oz Sugar
60 g/ 2 oz Grated coconut
Plain yogurt
(1 small container)
Shelled almonds,
or pistachio nuts for trim

30 g/ 1 oz Butter

For the syrup:
150 g/ 6 oz Sugar
1 Lemon

Servings: 4-6
Preparation time:20'+2/3h
Cooking time: 1h 10'
Difficulty: ●●
Flavor: ●
Kcal (per serving): 1005
Proteins (per serving): 27
Fats (per serving): 39
Nutritional value: ●●●

400 g/ 14 oz Semolina	**Servings: 4-6**	**Fats (per serving): 25**
150 g/ 6 oz Sugar	**Preparation time: 30′**	**Nutritional value: ●●●**
1 Packet baking powder	**Cooking time: 20′**	
2 Whole eggs +1 white	**Difficulty: ●●**	
Vanilla extract	**Flavor: ●●**	
40 g/ 1½ oz Butter	**Kcal (per serving): 706**	
Olive oil	**Proteins (per serving): 17**	

GHORIBA

Semolina cakes

1

2

3

4

1 Beat the yolks together with 100 g/ 4 oz sugar until thick and creamy. Dissolve the baking powder in a little lukewarm water and melt the butter.

2 Beat the egg whites until stiff, and gradually add the yeast, butter, a drop of olive oil, and a drop of vanilla extract.

3 Add the semolina to the egg whites and mix until malleable and homogeneous.

4 With your hands, make walnut-size balls, coat them with the remaining sugar and place them on a greased baking sheet; bake at 180 °C/ 350 °F for 20 minutes. Serve lukewarm.

Kibrizli

Almond cake

150 g/ 6 oz Farina
180 g/ 7 oz Sugar
120 g/ 5 oz Shelled almonds
Baking powder (1/2 packet)
5 Eggs, separated
1 Lemon
Salt
Sesame seeds

For the syrup:
1 Lemon
Honey

Servings: 4
Preparation time: 40′
Cooking time: 50′
Difficulty: ●●
Flavor: ●●
Kcal (per serving): 711
Proteins (per serving): 29
Fats (per serving): 27
Nutritional value: ●●●

1

2

3

4

1 Beat the egg yolks with the sugar until creamy, blend in the grated lemon zest, the farina, finely ground almonds, the baking powder and 1 glass water.

2 Beat the whites until stiff, with a pinch of salt, and then gently turn them into the yolk mixture.

3 Pour the batter into a greased round baking pan, lined with paper. Sprinkle the sesame seeds on top and bake at 180 °C/ 350 °F for 45 minutes.

4 Ten minutes before the cake is done, heat 3 tablespoons honey and simmer for 4 minutes. Remove from the stove and blend in the lemon juice. Pour the syrup over the cake, let it cool and then turn it out onto a serving dish.

KAAB AL GHAZAL

"Gazelle horns"

1

2

1 Soften the butter and blend in the finely chopped almonds, the sugar, 1 teaspoon ground cinnamon, and 2 tablespoons orange flower oil. Make little cylinders, about 5-6 cm (2/ 2½ inches) long and 1,5 cm (½ inch thick).

2 Knead the flour with a pinch a salt and ½ liter/ 2 cups lukewarm water, until you have an elastic dough; roll it out and cut strips 10 cm (4 inches) wide.

400 g/ 14 oz Flour 120 g/ 5 oz Sugar 300 g/ 12 oz Shelled almonds Ground cinnamon Orange flower oil, 50 g/ 2 oz Butter	Confectioner's sugar, for decoration Salt	**Servings: 4-6** **Preparation time: 40′** **Cooking time: 15′** **Difficulty: ●●** **Flavor: ●●** **Kcal (per serving): 931** **Proteins (per serving): 31**	**Fats (per serving): 42** **Nutritional value: ●●●**

3 Place the almond cylinders on top of the strips, and fold them in half; press down to seal the edges.

4 Use a pastry cutter to trim the outer edge and curve the "Gazelle horns" into a crescent. Place them on a buttered baking sheet and bake at 160 °C/ 325 °F for 15 minutes. Remove from the oven, and sprinkle with orange flower oil and confectioner's sugar.

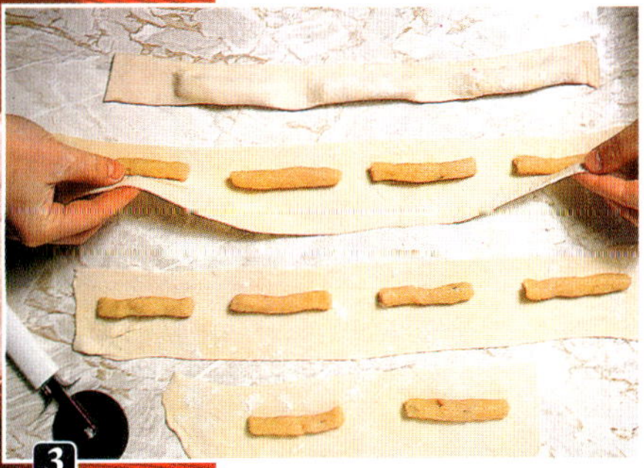
3

4

MAKROUD

Date lozenges

1

2

3

4

1 Combine 5 tablespoons olive oil and a pinch of salt with the semolina; gradually add lukewarm water to make a thick dough. Set aside for 15 minutes. Knead, then set aside for another 30 minutes.

2 Pit the dates and put them through the blender, add 1 tablespoon olive oil and 1 teaspoon ground cinnamon.

3 Roll out the dough thickly (about 1,5 cm/ ½ inch) and cut strips 6-7 cm (2 inches) wide.

4 Shape the chopped dates into cylinders, and place one on each strip of dough, fold over and cut the *makrouds*, shaping them into flat lozenges. Fry them in hot oil and drain on a paper towel. Dissolve the sugar in a saucepan with 1 glass water and the juice of the lemon; simmer until the syrup thickens. Remove from the stove and cool to lukewarm; when the *makrouds* have cooled, dip them into the syrup.

250 g/ 8 oz Semolina
100 g/ 4 oz Fresh dates
100 g/ 4 oz Sugar
Ground cinnamon
Salt
Olive oil
Vegetable oil

For the syrup:
200 g/ 8 oz Sugar
1 Lemon

Servings: 4
Preparation time: 50′+45′
Cooking time: 30′
Difficulty: ●●●
Flavor: ●●
Kcal (per serving): 894
Proteins (per serving): 7
Fats (per serving): 36
Nutritional value: ●●●

M'HENCHA

Almond twists

- 160 g/ 8 Sheets of *phyllo* dough (or very thin flake pastry)
- 500 g/ 1 lb. Shelled almonds
- 150 g/ 6 oz Honey
- Orange flower oil
- 80 g/ 3 oz Sugar
- Ground cinnamon
- 1 Egg
- 70 g/ 3 oz Butter
- Olive oil

Servings: 4-6
Preparation time: 45'
Cooking time: 35'
Difficulty: ●●
Flavor: ●●
Kcal (per serving): 1099
Proteins (per serving): 22
Fats (per serving): 83
Nutritional value: ●●●

Melt the butter, take half and combine with the almonds and put them through the blender along with the sugar, 1 teaspoon cinnamon and 1 teaspoon orange flower oil, to make a workable paste. Spread egg white on the sheets of dough and line them up, so that the edge of one overlaps the next. Shape the almond paste into a long sausage and place in the middle of the dough, fold the dough over making a sort of tube that you can twist into a spiral. Grease a round oven pan with olive oil, put the dough into it and brush with the remaining melted butter.

Bake at 170 °C/ 340 °F for 30 minutes. In the meantime, heat the honey over a low flame. When the cake is done, spread the liquefied honey over it.

YMM'ALI

Fruit cake

320 g/ 16 Sheets of *phyllo* dough (or very thin flake pastry)
60 g/ 2 oz Raisins
100 g/ 4 oz Shelled almonds
100 g/ 4 oz Shelled pistachio nuts
Honey
Cardamom
Ground cinnamon
Heavy cream, milk
75 g/ 3 oz Sugar
Olive oil

Servings: 4
Preparation time: 15'
Cooking time: 30'
Difficulty: ●●
Flavor: ●●
Kcal (per serving): 791
Proteins (per serving): 26
Fats (per serving): 59
Nutritional value: ●●●

Place the sheets of dough on a baking sheet, separating them with slightly greased oven paper, and bake at 170 °C/ 340 °F for 15 minutes.
When they are crisp, crumble them into an oven dish alternating with the raisins, and the chopped almonds and pistachio nuts. Over a low flame, combine 1 glass cream, 2 glasses of milk, the sugar, 1 tablespoon ground cardamom and 2 tablespoons honey.
Heat the mixture to the boil and then pour it over the contents of the baking dish, sprinkle with ground cinnamon and bake at 220 °C/ 425 °F for 10 minutes. Serve immediately.

Hilb bil Luz

Almond milk

125 g/ 5 oz Shelled almonds
1½ liters/ 1 ½ quarts Milk
120 g/ 5 oz Sugar
Orange flower oil

Servings: 4
Preparation time: 10'+1h
Cooking time: 5'
Difficulty: ●●
Flavor: ●
Kcal (per serving): 509
Proteins (per serving): 24
Fats (per serving): 24
Nutritional value: ●●●

1

2

1 Put the almonds through the blender and then put them into a little cheesecloth sack.

2 Pour the milk into a saucepan and dilute it with ½ liter/ 2 cups water, and dip the sack into it. Let it soak for one hour, every now and then, press down on the sack with a wooden spoon. Then, squeeze it out over the pan.

3 Now, slowly heat the milk, be careful not to let it boil, add the sugar and stir.

4 Remove the pan from the stove and add 2 teaspoons orange flower oil and stir. Serve the almond milk cold, it is an excellent, refreshing summer beverage.

3

4

'ASAL WA KUZBARA

Honey and coriander

Boil 3 dl/ 1 ½ cups water. Put 2 teaspoons honey and ½ teaspoon coriander seeds into each cup, (the best thing would be to crush the seeds in a mortar and reduce them to a fine powder). Pour on the boiling water, stir and serve. This is a beverage that warms you up, and thanks to the honey, is a wonderful home remedy for colds. The coriander also helps the digestive process, eliminating that heavy feeling after meals.

Coriander seeds, finely ground
Honey (acacia or mille fleur)

Servings: 4
Preparation time: 5'
Cooking time: 5'
Difficulty: ●
Flavor: ●●
Kcal (per serving): 10
Proteins (per serving): 0
Fats (per serving): 0
Nutritional value: ●

1 Peel the potato, mash it and combine it with the flour and pinch of salt, the yeast diluted in lukewarm water. Gradually add the milk which should be at room temperature.

HALOUA CHEBBAKIA

Honey fritters

2 Cover the bowl and set aside to rise for 1 hour. Knead it again, and set it aside to rise for another hour.

3 Shape little balls and fry them in hot oil; drain on paper towels.

4 Heat the honey in a sauce pan, dip the fritters into the softened honey and then roll them in the sesame seeds.

250 g/ 8 oz Flour
1 Potato, boiled in the jacket
20 g/ 1 oz Brewer's yeast
100 g/ 4 oz Sesame seeds
1 Glass milk
150 g/ 6 oz Honey
Vegetable oil for frying

Servings: 4
Preparation time: 45'+2h
Cooking time: 40'
Difficulty: ●●
Flavor: ●●
Kcal (per serving): 692
Proteins (per serving): 8
Fats (per serving): 28
Nutritional value: ●●●